The *Easy* Ice Skating Book

The *Easy* Ice Skating Book

by Jonah and Laura Kalb

Illustrated by Sandy Kossin

Houghton Mifflin Company   Boston   1981

For Joyce Underwood Winship

Library of Congress Cataloging in Publication Data
Kalb, Jonah.
    The easy ice skating book.
    Summary: An introduction to the equipment and basic
techniques of ice skating.
    1. Skating—Juvenile literature. [1. Ice skating]
I. Kalb, Laura. II. Title.
GV849.K28   796.91   81-6228
ISBN 0-395-31605-7   AACR2

Printed in the United States of America

P 10 9 8 7 6 5 4 3 2 1

Introduction

Ice skating can be a lot of fun. When you skate for fun, you laugh a lot.

There are many kinds of skating. You can become a speed skater or a figure skater or a hockey player. But before you can begin any of those sports, you have to learn the beginnings. It is a good idea to learn the beginnings right.

This is an easy book about beginnings. It covers everything you can probably do in your first year on the ice.

It is about free skating — the kind of skating you sometimes see on TV. And you will need figure skates — the kind with the high boot and the toe pick on the front.

But it is also the beginnings for hockey players and speed skaters. And if you want to skate only for fun, it has the only lessons you will ever need.

Before the Ice

Fitting Skates

Wear thin socks or tights when fitting figure skates. Put both boots on.

Lace the bottom two eyes loosely. Then lace tightly up to the bend at your ankle. Make a half knot at the ankle. Then lace the rest of the boot loosely again. Three finger tips should fit between the top of your boot and your leg.

Stand up. You should be able to wiggle your toes in both boots. Also, your toes should lie flat on the bottom of the sole. If they are squeezed up or if you can't wiggle, the boots are too small.

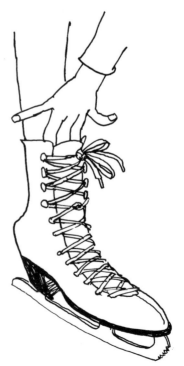

If the toes are okay, step on the back of one blade with the other, keeping the skate down. Then try to lift your heel inside the boot. Your heel should not come up more than one-half inch. If it does, the boots are too big. Try the same test on the other heel.

Stand up. See if the boots hug the sides of your feet snugly, also without squeezing. If that is okay, too, then the boots fit.

Getting Used to Your Skates

New skates have to be broken in. Breaking in will hurt your feet. It can't be helped. Everybody's new skates hurt.

The best way to break in new skates is to wear them around the house. Keep the skate guards on the blades, or you will scratch the floors and nick the blades.

Lace up your skates as if you were going on the ice. Wear them for about an hour at a time. Wear them

while watching TV. You don't have to walk all the time. Just wear them.

If you can, try to wear them about five times before you try them on the ice. Do some deep knee bends, holding on to the back of a chair. Don't loosen the laces. Try to bend the leather to your foot.

If you get blisters, you should get them only at the top of the boot where it rubs and in front of your ankles where you are bending the leather. The blisters will soon become calluses and won't hurt any more.

What to Wear on the Ice

Never go on the ice without gloves or mittens. You
will fall a lot. You will catch yourself with your
hands. Your hands will hurt a lot less if you are
wearing gloves or mittens. Bring two pairs. One
will get wet.

You should wear clothing in layers. Three sweaters
are better than one warm jacket. The reason is that
as you skate you will get warmer. You will want to
take something off. It is better to take off one
sweater than to take off the only jacket you are
wearing.

You should wear warm pants. Except when they are skating before large audiences, even Olympic skaters wear leg warmers or warm pants. Warm pants keep your muscles loose. They also protect you when you fall.

Remember, no matter what you wear, your feet will be cold.

Girls should not wear thin skating dresses until they are very good skaters and can keep warm just by skating fast.

First Day on the Ice

Falling

Everybody on skates falls every day. Hockey stars. Figure skating champions. Everybody. So the very first thing you must learn is how to fall.

The trick is — relax. Become a wet noodle. Wet noodles never get hurt.

Take off your skate guards. Then go on the ice and sit down. Let your feet slide in front of you and fall down. Then turn over on your hands and knees and get up again.

Sit down again. Get up. Sit down again. Get up.

Dive forward on your hands and knees and fall forward. Get up and do it again. Then fall backward again. Practice being a wet noodle.

If you stop being afraid to fall, then you can learn to skate.

If you forget to take your skate guards off, you will have a surprising fall. That's the worst kind. Everybody does it once. Then they remember.

Bending Your Knees

After falling, the most important thing to learn in skating is bending your knees.

Hold on to the boards at the side of the rink and practice bending your knees. Bounce up and down on them. Do deep knee bends and bends not so deep. Let go of the boards and do some more. Bounce a little.

Then, with your arms held out for balance, try marching in place. Pick up one foot and then the other. Bend your knees. March in place. Don't try to go anywhere yet.

You will probably fall. The reason you will fall is that while marching in place you forgot to bend your knees. Pick yourself up and do it again.

When you can march in place without falling, try to march forward. Again you will probably fall. You will lean forward and then lean back and lose your balance and fall. But you already know how to fall, so it doesn't hurt.

Then take three short steps forward and glide. Bend your knees. Glide on both feet.

Gliding

After you have practiced three steps and a glide, try five steps and a longer glide. See if you can cross the rink with just two long glides.

Now comes a hard part. Somewhere in the middle of a long glide, lift one of your feet and then put it down again. Next time, lift your other foot. Try lifting one, then the other, foot for longer and longer periods. See if you can make half your glide on just one foot.

Notice how you shift your weight when you glide on one foot? You have to shift your weight forward, over the ball of your foot, and sideways, directly over the blade that is on the ice. And you have to bend your knee.

If you fall backward, your weight is too far back on your heels. Lean forward. If you catch your toe pick and fall forward, you're not bending your knee enough.

If you have trouble balancing, get a chair. Turn it seat forward, so you can skate behind it holding the back. Push it across the ice in front of you while gliding on one foot, then gliding on the other.

Step, step, glide. Step, step, glide. You're almost skating.

Time Out Number One

Leave the ice. You have had enough for one day. But before you take your first step, put those skate guards on. Some rinks have rubber mats so you can walk on them without skate guards.

Don't do it. The mats are dirty. They will dull your blades. Put your skate guards on every time you leave the ice.

In the locker room, wipe your skates dry. Wipe everything that is metal, all the way up to the boot. Do not put your guards back on. Guards are for walking. They are probably still wet and will rust your blades if you leave them on.

Hold one boot upside down, heel to your chin, and aim it toward the light. Look down the skate blade. You should see two very important things about the blade.

First, looking down the length, you should see that the blade is not really flat. It is a gentle curve. That curve allows you to shift your weight back and forth, rocking on the blade without digging into the ice.

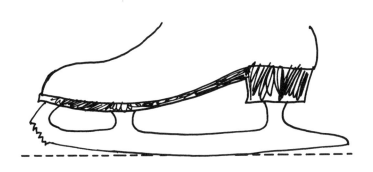

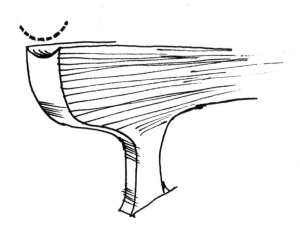

Second, looking at the blade side to side, you should see that the bottom isn't really flat either. There is a tiny curve dug out between two sharp edges. These edges are very important. There is an inside edge and an outside edge on every blade.

Strokes and Stops

Forward Stroking

Forward stroking is exactly like gliding without the steps in between.

Place your feet in a T position. Your left foot points forward. Your right foot, just behind your left foot, points sideways.

Put your arms out for balance. Bend both knees. Push hard on your back skate and glide on your front one.

Bring your right foot up parallel to your left. Turn your left foot outward, and then push hard on your left, gliding on your right.

Every push should be backward and to the side. Use the whole side of the blade when pushing. Don't push with your toe pick. Your weight must be forward over the ball of the gliding foot.

Notice that you cannot push unless your knee is bent. And the gliding foot is always under a bent knee.

Start with short strokes. Then make them longer.

Stopping

There are several stops that skaters learn. The easiest one is falling. Don't laugh. It works. But now that you know how to stroke, you'd better learn how to stop, too.

The Snow Plow is one of the stops you should learn. While going forward, glide on both skates. Bend your knees more than normally. Turn your toes in and your heels out. At the same time, push your skates sideways and dig in.

Just pointing your toes together will not make this stop. In fact, you will probably just fall forward. What you must do is push hard on your inside edges, moving them outward.

Another stop is called the T stop. Glide forward on one foot. Place the other foot right behind the forward skate, pointing sideways. It is just like the T at the beginning of the forward stroke. Lean backward. Shift weight back. Then dig the back skate into the ice. Push hard on the entire outside edge of the back skate.

If you don't lean backward, you will find yourself dragging your back foot. Dragging may stop you, also.

Sculling and Backward Stroking

To start sculling backward, bend your knees. Put your toes together and point your heels out. You are going to make a circle on the ice in front of you.

First, push your heels out. Then pull your heels in. Just before the heels touch, turn your toes in and heels out again. Bend your knees. Push your heels out and pull them in again. Do it again and again.

You get power to scull from pushing and from pulling both heels. You are always on your inside edges.

Backward stroking begins the same way as backward sculling. Toes are together. Heels are apart. Knees are bent. Arms are out.

You push forward and to the side with one of
your skates, gliding backward with the other.
You then bring your feet together, toes in, heels
out, and push forward and to the side with the
other skate.

When you push forward and to the side, you
leave your leg <u>ahead</u> of your body until you are
ready for the next stroke. Keep your hands out,
palms down.

After you learn backward crossovers, you will
probably never use either of these strokes again.

More Stops

One easy way to stop while skating backward is
to lean forward and let your toe picks dig into
the ice. You still have to bend your knees. It isn't
a fast stop, but it gets the job done.

Hockey stops, on the other hand, are very fast.
Skaters should learn Hockey stops left and
right.

While skating forward, quickly turn your hips and both skates to the right. Lean back with knees bent. Dig in on both blades, hard. You will be scraping the ice with the inside edge of your left skate and the outside edge of your right. This is a Hockey stop right.

A Hockey stop left is exactly opposite. Turn hips and both skates left. Lean back. Bend knees. Dig in with the inside edge of your front skate and the outside edge of your back skate.

A lot of skaters use a one-footed Hockey stop by twisting hips, bending knees, leaning back, but only using the inside edge of the lead skate to stop. That's fancy.

Crossovers

Forward Crossovers

Curving around the ice comes naturally to most skaters. When curving to the left, lead with your left foot, get on the outside edge of your left skate, shift weight left, and with bended knee, you naturally curve left.

Forward crossovers are a way to get powerful strokes while curving.

Start with one or two forward strokes to get yourself moving. Then get on the outside edge

of your left skate and glide. Twist your hips left
into the circle. Turn your head into the circle.
Pull your left arm back, elbow bent, palm down.
Put your right arm across your body, shoulder
forward. You will be curving left.

During the glide, bring your right skate forward and over your left skate. Bring your left
skate forward again on the outside edge. Stroke
with your right and glide. Do it again. Do it
again. Cross your right over your left. Stroke
with your right. Glide on your left. Hips left.
Head left. You've got it.

Backward Crossovers

Backward crossovers are the most important strokes in skating. It is from backward crossovers that almost every spin, almost every jump, and many moves are begun.

You begin learning backward crossovers by sculling backward. Toes together, heels apart, knees bent. Push out on your heels, then pull in on your heels.

Next, try backward sculling with only one foot. Keep your right foot on the ice, knee bent, and scull with your left foot only. Heel out, heel in.

You'll be curving backward and to the right.

Now, the body. While sculling with the left foot only, twist your body in the direction of the center of the circle. Pull your right shoulder back. Left arm across your body, left shoulder forward, head right.

Now, try half-sculling with your left skate. Push out on the heel, but don't pull in. Instead, lift your left skate and place it over the right skate. Uncross your feet by moving your right. Half-scull again with your left. Cross over with your left. Uncross. Half-scull. You are doing backward crossovers.

Time Out Number Two

As you just learned from crossovers, a lot of skating has nothing to do with skates. It has a lot to do with your body — your arms, your head, your hands, your elbows, and most important, your hips.

Moving your body in certain ways does more than make the skating beautiful. If you don't move your body, some moves are just impossible.

The real secret is in the hips. With your knees bent, your hips should be over the balls of your feet. If you want to get on one blade, as in gliding, you shift your weight over that skate by raising the opposite hip. If you want to turn, you twist your hips in the direction of the turn.

Except in special moves, your shoulders should always be over the hips. That keeps your back straight.

And you should keep your head up. You don't have to watch yourself skate.

Hips, shoulders, arms, and head must be in good position if you are going to look good, and if you are going to make the right moves the right way.

Moves

Shoot the Duck

The first fun move most skaters learn is called Shoot the Duck.

Skate forward until you build up speed. Then glide on both skates. Bend your knees very deeply. Lean forward, grab one of your ankles with both hands, lift that foot off the ice, and then sit down on your other heel.

You must keep your weight forward, especially when you sit down, or you will find yourself sitting on the ice, not on your heel.

Keep your free leg stiff, pointing straight ahead, holding it firmly off the ice with both hands.

Shoot the Duck backward is really the same. You just skate backward, getting good speed. Lift one foot forward and sit on your back skate.

Do a forward Shoot the Duck when skating with a friend. Put your arms up in the air and let the friend push. This is called Wheelbarrow.

Spirals

A Spiral is a long glide on one skate. Raise the back foot as high as you can. You can do a Spiral forward or backward, on either foot, on the flat of your blade, or on either edge. The Spiral will go straight or in a gentle curve. It is one of the best-looking moves on the ice.

To do a forward Spiral straight down the ice, you stroke up to fair speed and then glide on your stronger foot. Stretch your back leg as far back and as high as you can manage, keeping your head up.

Then, using your back, head, and leg as one unit, tilt the top of your body forward until it is flat over the ice. Your back leg will, of course, go still higher. Hold your arms out, palms down, like the wings of an airplane.

Most skaters do Spirals on the outside edges of their skates. This gives a gentle curve to the glide. Start as if you're going straight. Then move your head in the direction of the curve and drop the shoulder on that same side. Keep your head up. Beautiful.

Lunges and Pivots

You have already done Lunges. You did them when you first tried to make a T stop, but your weight was forward. So you dragged your back skate. In the T stop, your weight has to be on the back skate.

The way to make a Lunge look like a good move is to stretch that back leg as far out as it will go. The way to do that is to deep knee bend the front leg. Keep your head up. Present your upper chest. Put your arms out at shoulder height. Keep your weight on your front skate and drag the back skate.

A nice way to come out of a Lunge is to slowly straighten your front leg, slowly pulling in your back leg. Then quickly shift your weight back and T stop.

There are front Pivots and back Pivots. This is how you do a front Pivot. Heels together, dig one toe pick into the ice and bend that knee. Arms out. Push the other skate out and forward, making a circle around your toe pick. If you push hard, you will go fairly fast. Keep all your weight over the skate with the toe pick in the ice. The outer skate is just gliding on the inside edge.

Three-Turns

There are all kinds of Three-Turns. Inside and outside Threes, forward and backward, either foot. They are very important, because they change your motion from skating forward to skating backward (or backward to forward) without losing speed.

It is hard to believe but the entire Three-Turn is managed by your arms. If you move your arms correctly, your skates will make the correct Three-Turn without your thinking about it.

It is called a Three-Turn because the figure carved on the ice by your blade is the number 3.

Glide on your left foot on the outside edge. Keep your right skate off the ice. Left knee bent. You are making a gentle curve left. Arms out.

Now, pretend you are holding a stick in your hands. Look to the left in the direction of the curve and move both arms (still on the stick) far to the left. Move them at the same time.

One final push farther left and then jerk your arms all the way to the right. Don't move your head. Let the jerk of your arms move your skates. You will end up on an inside edge, skating backward.

Spins

Two-Foot Spins

Spinning on the ice is one of the best-looking moves you can make. It is also fairly easy to do, but it looks hard. Everybody likes to spin.

The Two-foot Spin is easiest. With your weight over the balls of your feet as always, you just wind your body up, twisting your hips, waist, shoulders, head, and arms to one side. Knees bent.

Then, as hard as you can, you throw your arms out, straightening your knees at the same time. Your arms are then brought to your front as if you were holding a big balloon. Finally, you

bring your arms to your chest as your spin slows down.

The trick is, wind yourself up to one side with everything, and bend those knees. Then, in one violent motion, untwist, throw your arms out, spring your legs up, and spin. Stay on the flats of your blades.

While spinning, you must stand straight up. Don't lean or get on an edge, or you will wobble.

One-Foot Spins

The best way to start a One-Foot Spin is from a Pivot. Remember the Pivot? You dig the toe pick into the ice, bend the knee, and push out with the other foot. In the Pivot, you shift your weight over the toe pick and drag the other foot wide.

In the One-Foot Spin, you wind your body up just as in the Two-Foot Spin — head, arms, shoulders, waist, hips all to one side. Dig the opposite toe pick into the ice. Bend the knee. Push out hard with your other foot. That starts you spinning in a Pivot.

Then you do four things at the same time.

First, you throw your arms out and untwist.
Second, you get off the toe pick and get on the
flat of the blade. You keep your weight over the
ball of the spinning skate. Third, you pull your
outside leg in, lifting the skate off the ice. You
touch the boot of the free leg to the middle of
the spinning leg, holding it there. And fourth,
you straighten out the bent knee of the spinning foot.

If you do all four things at the same time, very
hard, after you are already spinning in a Pivot,

you will spin very fast. Then, again, move your arms as if circling a balloon in front of you and pull them in slowly to your chest.

Scratch Spins

Scratch Spins are the ones Olympic champions do. They can be done so fast the skater looks like a blur. They are a little harder to learn, but it's worth it.

You enter the Scratch Spin from backward crossovers. Do the crossovers in the same direction as clock hands move. You will, at one point, be on a back inside edge of your right skate, with your left leg stretched behind you.

From that position, you wind up your arms to
the right. Keep your head over your left shoulder. You then step forward with your left foot
twisted out, catching the ice with a deep outside
edge. Bend your left knee deeply. Your head, left
shoulder, and left hip are over your left knee,
but you are wound up anyway.

Lift and throw your right leg around to the
front of your body. At the same time, quickly

straighten your left knee, and throw your arms out. You are now spinning.

Your right leg, however, is now in front of you. Twist your right ankle outward and bring your foot in and across your left knee. At the same time, circle your arms in front as if holding the big balloon. Slowly lower your right foot to near the ice, bringing your arms in to your chest and then lowering your hands to below your waist. You are now spinning like a top.

Time Out Number Three

Here are some safety tips:

Sharp skates: Edges of ice skates, especially right after sharpening, are like razor blades. Since you must leave the guards off or the blades will rust, you have to carry them carefully. Never run your finger on the edge of a blade to see if it is sharp. It is always sharp enough to cut your finger.

Others on the ice: You have to keep your eyes open and watch out. Remember, somebody in a jump or spin cannot watch out for you. You must keep out of the way.

Collisions: It's like riding a bike. Always figure the other person is going to make a mistake or not see you. Keep out of the way. Play it safe.

Getting up: Everybody falls. But don't just sit there on the ice very long either. If you are sitting on the ice, you can't get out of the way of a jumper or spinner.

Getting tired: Like all other sports, when you are tired, you are more likely to get hurt. If you are too tired, get off the ice and skate another day.

Spirals: Before doing Spirals, be extra careful. You are holding a very sharp blade three or four feet in the air. You don't want people running into it.

Jumps

Bunny Hop

The Bunny Hop is the first jump most skaters learn. It is a jump that starts face forward and ends face forward with no twists in the air. You take off on one foot and land on the other.

Skate forward to build up speed. Then glide on both skates. Lift your right foot off the ice and swing it back. Bring both arms back at the same time. Bend your left knee.

Swing your right leg forward at the same time that you swing both arms forward. Jump off the left skate by straightening the left knee.

As you jump, transfer your weight to your right side. Land on the right toe pick. Put your left skate down on the ice and push off the toe pick into a left-footed glide.

That's all there is to it. Swing the leg and the arms together. Straighten the take-off knee at the same time. Bend the landing knee. Land on the toe pick and push off quickly.

Waltz Jump

The Waltz Jump is harder than the Bunny Hop. You take off facing forward, and you land facing backward. You will do a half-turn with your body in the air. You will take off on one foot and land on the other.

Start with your feet in a T position, left skate leading, and push off with your right. After the push off, leave your right leg stretched behind you. Lead with your left shoulder. Look to the left over your shoulder. Hands out, palms down.

Without moving your head, swing both arms back and then swing both arms and your right

leg forward — hard. Spring off your left leg to
get some height.

Pretend you are jumping over a log on the ice.
Twist in the air by bringing your right arm
sharply around and forward. Land facing backward on the toe pick of your right skate. Lower
your heel to an outside edge. The knee is bent.

Then sharply pull your right arm back to stop
the rotation, leaving your left arm still forward.
Swing the left leg back, like a low Spiral.

That's it. The Waltz Jump.

Half-Flip

The Half-Flip is the easiest jump and uses the toe pick to lift you off the ice. You will take off facing backward and land facing forward on both skates. You will have to do a Three-Turn going into the jump.

Start with the T position, left skate in front, right skate to the side. Lead with your left shoulder. Push off with your right skate and glide forward on your left outside edge. You are curving slightly to the left.

Do a Three-Turn with the arms. Remember?
Look to the left. Move both arms as if you were
holding a stick, far to the left. Then jerk your
arms all the way to the right without moving
your head. Your arms move the skates.

You are now skating backward on the left inside
edge, and your right foot is dangling above the
ice behind you. Your left arm is in front of you,
right arm behind.

Dig your right toe pick into the ice hard and
straighten your bent knee. That will lift you
into the air. At the same time, throw your right
arm up and around your front, giving you the
twist in the air. Land on both skates, gliding
forward on bent knees, left arm forward and
right arm to the side.

You have just Half-Flipped.

Checking Out

As you do harder and harder jumps, you will see that you almost always land facing backward. Most skaters almost always land on the right skate and on the outside edge with the left leg behind as in a backward Spiral. The skater's arms are out, palms down, and the right knee — the landing knee — is in a deep bend.

That is the way most jumps are "checked out." When you land a jump after turning in the air, you have to stop the turning by pulling your right arm out and to the side, and throwing your left arm out and to the front.

You also land on your toe pick, but right after you hit the ice, you bend your knee. That gets you off the toe pick and onto the edge of your blade. A deep knee bend helps you hold the landing without falling.

The deep knee bend also makes the landing gentle. The outside edge holds the ice. The arms stop the turning.

Beautiful check outs are part of jumping and part of spinning, too. Checking out of spins uses the same arm and knee movements. All end up in a gentle backward Spiral.

End Piece

If you have done all the things in this book, it still is just the beginning.

There are many more moves, all beautiful. They have funny names, like Spread Eagles, Ina Bauers, and Mohawks.

There are wonderful spins called Camels, Laybacks, and Sit Spins. There are single, double, and sometimes triple jumps called Flips, Loops, Lutzes, and Axels. There are Russian Splits, Stags, and Mazurkas.

There is figure skating — carving circles and loops and turns in the ice. Some skaters find that fun.

Then there is hockey. It's a great game.

There is speed skating and pair skating and ice dancing.

To learn these and do everything well takes hundreds of hours of lonely practice. For those heading for the Olympics, it may be worth it. But for most of you, the quiet pond on a winter day or a Friday evening with a friend at the rink is all you really want.

Friendship and skating. They go together.

About the Authors

Jonah and Laura Kalb, father and daughter, bring complementary talents to this book for beginning ice skaters.

Jonah Kalb is author of The Kids' Candidate, The Goof That Won the Pennant, The Easy Baseball Book, The Easy Hockey Book, and with Dr. David Viscott, What Every Kid Should Know — all published by Houghton Mifflin. He is a graduate of Oberlin College and is a business consultant.

Laura Kalb is a Phi Beta Kappa graduate of Skidmore College, a teacher of beginning skating to groups and private students, and was a gold medalist free-style skater in the 1972 Lake Placid competitions. Alas, it was not the Olympics. This is her first book.